READING POWER

Extreme Machines

Monster Trucks

Scott P. Werther

The Rosen Publishing Group's
PowerKids Press™
New York

Published in 2002 by The Rosen Publishing Group, Inc.
29 East 21st Street, New York, NY 10010

First Edition

Book Design: Victoria Johnson

Photo Credits: Cover © AFP/Corbis; pp. 4–5, 9, 13, 14–15, 17–21 © Bigfoot 4x4 Inc.; pp. 6–7 © Watson/The Image Works; pp. 10–11 © J. Froscher/The Image Works

Thanks to Bigfoot 4X4, Inc.

Werther, Scott P.
Monster trucks / by Scott P. Werther.
     p. cm. — (Extreme machines)
Includes bibliographical references and index.
ISBN 0-8239-5955-4 (library binding)
1. Monster trucks—Juvenile literature. [1. Monster trucks. 2. Trucks.] I. Title.
TL230.15 .W48 2001
796.7—dc21
                                                2001001730

Manufactured in the United States of America

Contents

Monster Trucks

This is a monster truck. Monster trucks have very large tires. These trucks race and do special tricks.

The tires of monster trucks can be as tall as ten feet.

Monster trucks are very heavy.
They use very large engines
to help them move.

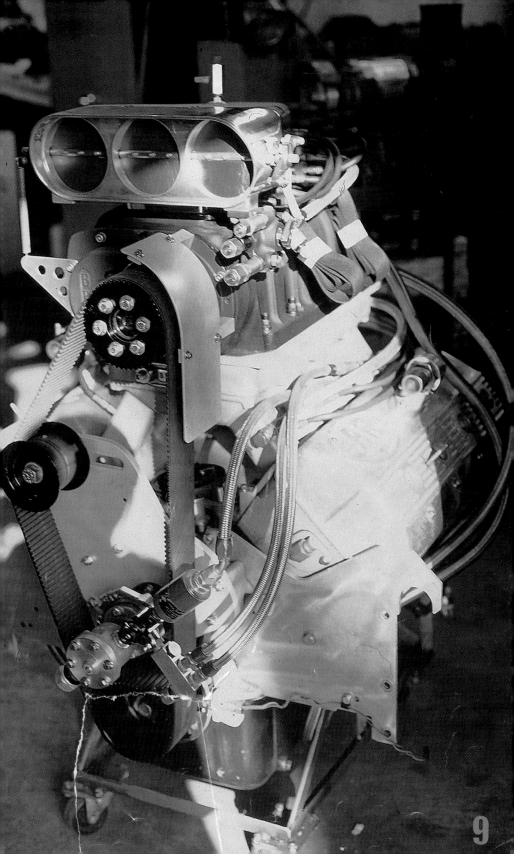

The body of a monster truck lifts up. This makes it easier for people to fix the engine.

Smooth Rides

Monster trucks use special springs and shock absorbers. The springs and shock absorbers make riding in a monster truck very smooth.

Shock
Absorber

Most monster trucks are very colorful. They have fancy paint jobs.

The Driver

Drivers wear hard helmets to keep safe. They also wear seat belts.

Helmet

Seat Belt

17

Special Tricks

Monster trucks can do tricks. They can even drive over other cars.

These monster trucks are racing each other. Monster trucks are as fun to watch as they are to drive.

Glossary

body (**bahd**-ee) the main part of a monster truck

engine (**ehn**-jihn) a machine that gives power to another machine

helmet (**hehl**-miht) a covering to protect the head

seat belt (**seet behlt**) a strap used to hold people steady in their seats

shock absorber (**shahk** uhb-**sorb**-uhr) a device that helps make a car or truck ride smoother

springs (**sprihngz**) a coil of metal or plastic that returns to its original shape after it is pulled or pushed

tires (**tyrz**) thick, round rubber coverings that go around the wheels of a vehicle

tricks (**trihks**) clever acts of skill

Resources

Books

Monster Machines
by Caroline Bingham
Dorling Kindersley Publishing (1998)

Monster Trucks
by James Koons
Capstone Press (1996)

Web Site

http://www.reptoid.com

Index

Word Count: 137

Note to Librarians, Teachers, and Parents

If reading is a challenge, Reading Power is a solution! Reading Power is perfect for readers who want high-interest subject matter at an accessible reading level. These fact-filled, photo-illustrated books are designed for readers who want straightforward vocabulary, engaging topics, and a manageable reading experience. With clear picture/text correspondence, leveled Reading Power books put the reader in charge. Now readers have the power to get the information they want and the skills they need in a user-friendly format.